MW00637229

Magic Crayons

Magic Crayons

POEMS AND ESSAYS

Maylie Donaldson

Maylie Donaldson

March 7, 2012

Donaldson Enterprises
Redmond, Washington

MAGIC CRAYONS
Copyright © 2011 by Maylie Ward Donaldson
First Printing, August 2011

All rights reserved. No part of this book may be used
or reproduced in any manner whatsoever without
written permission except in the case of brief quotations
embodied in critical articles and reviews.

Published by University Book Store Press
Printed on the Espresso Book Machine
4326 University Way NE
Seattle, WA 98105
www.ubookstore.com

ISBN 13: 978-1-937358-00-6
ISBN 10: 1-937358-00-3

Manufactured in the United States of America

First Edition

For my parents
Merrill and Dorothy Ward

CONTENTS

Magic Crayons

My Father's Crayons

My Father brought home crayons

fifty four bright colors   in shiny flat black boxes

a white Old Faithful geyser on the top

Prang crayons

from his large sample suitcases

with long straps and metal buckles

manila paper substantial beige

he tore the wrapping off the ream

five hundred sheets.

Less than two years old on baby hands and knees

favorite orange crayon scribbling marks

in all directions.

Four years old squirming in church

God talking too loud too long

Father quietly giving me paper and a pen

I draw God giving the benediction.

A warm summer Sunday morning in our small country church

window open behind the piano

my feet swinging back and forth hands fidgeting

my Father gives me paper and crayons.

God wears a black suit a red tie

large green potted palms surround his feet

rooster in an apple tree crowing praises

from whom all blessings flow

I fly out the window with magenta wings.

Aluminum Cans

My Father collected aluminum cans
in the park where people left them
he walked every day.

The teenagers called him "Mr. Clean."
One day my Mother was with him
they said, "and here comes Mrs. Clean."

My father sold the aluminum cans
sent the money to Petey Annon
a friend from high school
who had been in a wheelchair for sixty years
           since his father beat him.

After Petey died my Father
gave the money to a grandmother
in the next condominium to buy a bicycle
for the twelve year old grandson
she was raising alone.

My Father collected aluminum cans
in the park where people left them.

The Painting

My Father brought home a painting
he bought from the artist
I asked my Mother what it was a painting of
sitting down in front of me holding the painting
                                        smiling
she asked what I thought it was a painting of
standing in front of her   nine years old
                    I studied a red square
on the same line to the right
a smaller blue rectangle
dark Prussian blue surrounded each shape
and filled the background
            I didn't know.
Laughing   laughing   laughing
she could hardly speak
she whispered   "The Washing."

I am going to do a painting of the washing
to hear my Mother laugh again.

My Mother's Threes

Sometimes when I make a three
it looks just like the threes
my Mother used to make
round precise deliberate
artistic with little flags
at the beginning and the end.

I like making threes that look like my Mother's
unintentionally recreating her threes
from fifty   sixty years ago even seventy years ago
before I was born she made threes carefully
                         with a holy intentness
a certain push and placement of her pen
that formed consistent half circles.
I could depend on them to be strong
to be different from everyone else's.

My Mother

I took my Mother to the beach today
and two of her handkerchiefs
white rolled scalloped edges
one gray with large red peonies green leaves
the other blue with red and yellow roses
                              green rose leaves.
We watched the sky change gray to blue
rain moved out to sea
clouds gathered along the horizon
the sun joined us.
Between snow rain hail we built an alter
                    to the Ocean and our life together
placed on it driftwood   red cedar   round   wet   crumbling
kelp rubbery green brown leaves and stem
a gray heart shaped stone
a reddish brown stone the shape of two women
                         standing side by side

another stone a dark tear drop

a wet sparkling black half moon stone

one more stone gray on one side

white on the other even melted

fused together in the center

all of the stones polished by each other.

I dropped a mitten

we went back and found it.

For My Mother

No no it wasn't me
I had a happy childhood   Mother saw to that
scraping frost off the hall window with a spoon
the winter we had no heat upstairs.
Wearing a red Kladezee snow suit with three zippers
one long one up the front   a shorter one on each leg
belt attached at the sides that buckled easily with a twist
matching red helmet like Amelia Earhart's.
We drew pictures in the heavy frost on the windows
snowing too hard to play outside.

It was my Mother
who lost the four most important men
in her life in one year when she was too young
to know about death but too old to grieve.

Her father John Ransome Williams
 "Ross"   "Papa"   my grandfather
ran away from home when he was sixteen
carried the flag in the Confederate Army
fought for his family's plantation on the James River
graduated from Asbury Academy   swam the Columbia River.

Married Marian Lenore Hickey "Molly"   "Mama"
my grandmother when she was twenty
    and he was forty.

Her older brother   Albert Williams
injured in a mine accident   an elevator came down on him
    broke his back
they brought him home in a wheelbarrow
    thought he was dead
Mama   my grandmother nursed him back to life
told my Mother he was never quite right after that
he couldn't remember.

Her little cousin Nelson
died of tuberculosis when he was eleven
he had slept in the same bed with his mother
who died of it
Mama my grandmother raised him.

Her grandfather   James Hickey   Mama's father
my great grandfather   left Ireland when he was sixteen
thought he would not like his stepmother

lived with my mother's family Papa and Mama
Who would support them?   She did.
My Mother finished high school when she was sixteen
rode the streetcar into Chicago to work
giving her Mother all of her paycheck
helping to send her brother Paul to college
"because boys have to earn the living".
Mama giving her streetcar money.

No no it wasn't my grief
it was my mother's
I kept it for her in the pockets of my red Kladezee snowsuit.

For my Mother, Dorothy Ross Williams Ward
                 b. August 24, 1895
                 d. Jan. 25, 1980
and my Grandmother, Marian Lenore Hickey Williams
                 Molly   Mama
        b. 1864
        d. 1936

God Lived

When I was very small
every time we went downtown
we passed a small stone building
    on the edge of a large cemetery.

    I thought God lived
in the small dark stone building
with its gray slate roof
a short narrow wooden door
only one window with four rippled panes
    reflections
        wobbled in the glass as we drove past.

There were trees on each side
hugging the small stone building
behind it as far as I could see
were trees and flowers
    statues
        and square standing stones.

    I thought God lived
in the small stone building
with trees and flowers
    statues and stones.

The Pond

Going home to twilight
light enough in the backyard
to see the white anemones   blue flax
purple violets between the large stones
placed around the edge of the handmade fish pond
a hole scooped out of the ground
cement mixed in a wheelbarrow
placed by the shovelful
over the slanting earth
smoothed with a trowel.

We played in the pond
the summer of the polio epidemic
when we couldn't leave our yard.
With a bucket and a broom
my Father removed the rain water
                    and leaves
scrubbed the cement
added buckets of hot water
we held the hose Peggy and I
cold water mixed with hot water
from the buckets my Father
carried from the kitchen
the water reached the rim of the pond
    the stones the purple violets
      two little girls
          sat in the middle splashing
              waves dashed to the shore.

Armistice Day, November 11, 1940

We watched the snow, all day we watched the snow
pile up in drifts next to the house, across the front yard,
the road, the fields across the road. From the second story
windows we watched the dark sky and the fierce wind blow
the snow in sheets pelting the windows until the glass shook.

We tried to settle down to play but we interrupted
each other by going to the windows to watch the snow drifting
deeper and higher, the wind that never stopped. We went
from the windows in our bedroom to the window in the hall,
then to my brother's bedroom windows. We had never seen
such a storm. It was afternoon but it looked like the middle
of the night.

We put on our snow suits. We knew we could not go
outside but we needed to be dressed appropriately, for the
fury outside had taken over and what we watched through
the windows seemed to come inside. We put on our helmets
to quiet the roaring and whistling of the wind. We wore our
mittens and borrowed spoons from the kitchen to scrape the
frost off the inside of the windows so we could eat it. It was
the only food left.

My brother explained snow survival but my sister and I were not listening. We were lost. We were with Admiral Byrd and his dogs at the South Pole. We had seen his dogs at a Purina Dog Food promotion and they were our trusted companions. They would know the way. They would take us where we needed to go. They would share their food. When we needed to rest they would keep us warm with their body heat while the wind covered us with snow like an igloo. They would rescue us. We would survive.

Dear Little Sister

We were mothers in the cave the winter
of the great freeze   snow   ice covered the land
driving the men long days away to find food
we kept the fire burning   the children fed
the old people alive   by drawing on the walls of the cave.
We drew   chanted   prayed   survived.

Dear little Sister   thirteen months younger   five inches taller
we shared rooms in every cave we shared a room
two cribs in the white house in St. Louis Park
twin beds in the brown stucco house at 129 Blake Road
one on each side of the room
twin beds pushed together barely room to walk around
at 4007 Zenith Avenue South   bunk beds on Bryant Avenue.

Never having had a room of our own we married
you first no longer only ourselves now all things to another
work eight hours a day   keep house   cook   shop   socialize
study   learn   keep learning   to stop is to die
you will suffocate   in the rooms of clothes to be washed
meals to be cooked   suffocate in the endlessness
of clean   cook   wash   feed   nurse   teach.
                    We replenished
the draining away with our needlework   clay
paints   crayons   pencil   pen   longing   searching

        for something beyond   and something within

            we drew on the walls of the cave.

Footsteps

When I was growing up
  our summer lawns held the footsteps
  of my Mother who planted petunias
  my Father who gave us his smiling blue eyes
  my Sister Jody five years older
    who taught us laughing is fun
  my Brother Jamie two years older
    who taught me to study
  my Sister Peggy thirteen months younger
    whom I protected
  our dog Dinah   black with brown eyebrows
  my Aunt Peg who brought orange slices on Thursday
  my Grandma Molly who sang to us
    and rocked us to sleep.

We moved but the grass stayed the same
         soft green growing.
Our footsteps changed
  from small baby shoes
  passed down from older to younger
    to sizes large enough to fit our teenage aspirations.

Our footsteps walked away to college

      to Montana   to Cambridge

      to New York   to California

        to sidewalks

             sand beaches

high mountains   studious brick buildings.

    Days turning into lifetimes

      lifetimes

         turning into

            poems.

Magic Crayons

Magic crayons   fifty two colors
in a long black and white box
        Prang crayons
carried with me from childhood
        to the present day.
I cannot be without them.
They tell me who I am and how I am feeling.

They understand what it is like
to move out of a house
we have lived in for thirty nine years.
They know what our gardens looked like in June
        the roses in bloom
in winter the helleborus magenta above the snow.
The trilliums surprising me.

They know what it feels like to say goodbye
to sixty fuchsia magellanica plants
propagated from one plant given to me
                on a hot summer day.

They know when the children
are coming home   and when they are leaving.

They know when my sisters are ill.
                and when they are dying.

They tell me I will feel better
if I draw the tall dark green pine trees
in the woods around the new apartment building
and the blue violet sky   before the light fades.

Together

What does a child want from its mother?
    I felt like I gave them
        everything I had to give
        everything that was in me
    except the part I gave to their Father
        I drew him in to help me give to them
    was it enough   was it what they needed
    or what they needed but not what they wanted
        was the part they wanted
    the part of myself that wasn't there yet
    the part I was being taught by our life together
            the only place I could learn it

one breakfast	one lunch	one dinner
one story	one poem	one song
one sunrise	one sunset	one day

            one prayer   at a time?

Our Baby

If I awaken in the night
and there is no wind
        no rain
no one is coughing
no one is crying
I place my hand
on the baby inside me
I feel our baby's heart beating
soft   silken
       close against my hand
I fall asleep holding
our baby's heart beating.

Take The Guns Away

Written while watching the rising
of the full moon from our kitchen window
March 26, 1994 for Melissa Fernandes   age 16
who died March 24, 1994 a victim of gang violence.

Prayer for Melissa Fernandes   her Mother
and her Special Friend   Ryan Lam.

Moon in the arms of Pine Tree
take the guns away from the Children
while they sleep remove their weapons.

When my Brother was twelve years old
he bought a BB gun with his own money
he earned it caddying carrying golf clubs
for players at the nearby golf course.
My Father bought the BB gun from him
offered him twice the amount he'd paid for it
my Brother accepted his offer.
My Father threw the gun
into the cistern
lifted the iron cover with a crow bar
dropped it down into enough black water to drown it.

Moon in the arms of Pine Tree
take the guns from the Children.

The Saddest Day

It was the saddest day when my Mother died

it was a personal grief shared by my family

and this was the saddest day

it was a universal grief

shared by almost all the people on our planet

almost all the people in the world cried that day

the sadness was everywhere

in the light   the clouds   the wind

it was in the water   the rain   the air

the music   Beethoven's concertos   symphonies

oratorios   sounded heavier   older   deeper

clearer   sounded as if they were crying

as if they could not stop sobbing

as if all the people in the world

were overcome with grief

a grief that was too vast to bear

      too vast to ever go away

            which of course it never will.

September 11, 2001

In Memory

It could be our memorial to all the people
     who died on September 11,2001
     and in the rocket that exploded last week
     and all the people who have died
          who were not supposed to.
It could be our memorial
     we who were not in the Twin Towers
     or not trying to rescue the people who were
     we who have not been killed by drunken drivers
     or guns that are not supposed to be loaded.
I will dedicate my efforts to the twelve year old girl
     who was teased so much at school she hung herself
     in her room rather than go back to school the next day.
Our memorial would be to clean up America
     to clean up all the trash everywhere
          along the highways
               city streets
               railroad tracks
               beaches
               streams
               parks
               alleys
               vacant lots
               woods
               lakes
               oceans
     clean up and keep America clean
          in memory of all the people who have died
               who were not supposed to.

35

Memorial To September 11, 2001

Thank you America for picking up your trash.

I am so proud of you America

      for putting trash in it's place.

I am so proud of you!

      Thank you for using the waste baskets and

            garbage cans.

I am so proud of you America

      for picking up your trash!

Thank you America

      for keeping America clean!

Wings

Leave the day

     but take the wonder

     and escape to the sea.

Leave the time

     but take the heartfelt peace

     I give to thee.

Leave the people

     their cries   needs   expectations

     pounding on the door.

Leave and fly   soar

     dance with angels

     they have left their wings

       behind the door.

Our Paths

We made our own path

down the steep slope

holding hands and willow stems

we made a place next to Queen Anne's lace

to eat our sandwiches drink our V8

the bright warm early morning sun

the last of fall that made us plan this picnic lunch

had been replaced by dark blue clouds

wind whipped brown leaves around us

we talked about your morning dissecting in the anatomy lab

my morning working in the University Hospital

we watched

      below

         the river flowed.

We made our own path

along the grass and wildflower covered bank

sun setting behind the cliffs across the river

we found a place

surrounded by Queen Anne's lace

to eat our salmon pate bread cheese and wine

we talked about our day with Monet and his family

                                  at Giverny

in his studio   their house   their garden

walking along their nasturtium path

sitting by their lily pond

the fields beyond   behind

the poplar trees   cows

                   moving slowly.

You read the Wall Street Journal

you found it in Vernon

I walked along the river

gathered wildflower seeds

filled large patch pockets

of my blue denim skirt

       below the river flowed.

We made our own path along the creek

in the rain across slippery rocks to the statue

of Hiawatha carrying Minnehaha across the water

we touched her metal moccasins

his bow and arrows   his arms strong around her

this had been their land   their home   their woods

creek   and waterfall   we borrowed their place

to eat our lunch   we watched   below

the water flowed over the falls.

43

We made our own path

along the bank through the Scotch Broom

and the tall grasses to the edge of the lake

small waves breaking on the sand below

we sat down under a Madrona tree

legs dangling over the bank

feet resting on rocks below

we talked about your day working

in the University Hospital.

I had taken our youngest child to the airport

to go away   her first year of college

I came home packed our supper in the cooler

waited for you to go to the park

you were surprised and happy to leave

the empty house lonely in the late summer sun

we watched a Great Blue Heron

tease a black and white dog

by flying just out of reach offshore

across the lake hot air balloons

floating toward the mountains

Mt. Rainier turned from blue to pink

in the sun setting behind the Olympics

we listened   the water flowed

small waves breaking on the sand below.

1. Mississippi River, Minneapolis, Minnesota
2. The Seine River, Vernon, France
3. Minnehaha Creek and Falls, Minneapolis, MN
4. Lake Washington, Magnuson Park, Seattle, WA

46

What My Heart Wants To Know

Early fall school starts   begin again

begin anew   learn   write   remember

take yourself into books you have not read before

take yourself further along your path

listen   hear the fall wind   rain

see the heron return to rest all day in the tall pine tree

the sun moving further south   setting earlier   rising later

leaves changing color   yellow   orange   red   gold

notebooks filling with pages of notes

        books open to teach me,

art classes   writing classes   Buddhism   Spirit class

I am free to wonder   free to choose

  free to create my education

    free to explore without credits or grades

      without boundaries or restrictions

       free to find   honor   claim

        what my heart

          wants to know.

Collage Class

What I need to do:

    jar my thinking

    open the box of my mind

                look inside

    say mind,

        "We are moving to a new place."

Disturb my heart

    say heart

        " I love you   I want you big

    I   want   a   big

        big heart."

    peel off your petals

    give them away

    the clouds will collect them

49

the wind will bring them back

the trees will answer you when you ask.

the sky will wrap you in her blanket of blue

the ocean will share her peace

the waves will speak to your soul

      speak to your soul

        speak to your soul

          speak to your soul.

Poetry

Poetry came from silence
and the snow covered fields
ocean waves gliding
across the sun warmed sand   bare feet
at high tide crashing rocks rolling
a mother whale bringing her child circling close
we ate dinner watching from the cliff
mother and baby   rolling   laughing   feeding
sun setting   darkness led them south for the winter.

Poetry came from white suds on the floor
the brush scratching back and forth across it
making half circles lace designs of suds and water
knees pinched against the unrelenting floor
scrubbing the day away on the floor
out the door the river flowing.

Poetry came from deep crevasses of white snow
                                    blue mountains
a rainbow rising out of the lake
sunrise turning the face of the mountain orange
leaves   red   gold   purple
a horse galloping by rider calling
a cemetery at the base of the mountain
wildflowers between the graves.

Poetry came from moonlight shining
through the window on the wall
footprints in the snow across the frozen lake
a church steeple on the horizon
children laughing   playing   singing
lights on the Christmas tree   flowers fading
a train whistle across the lake
your smile raising your eyebrow
days forgotten   days remembered
                        and sixty six years.

Words

Words were there
      some clear   strong
      others   out of reach   amniotic
floating through clouds
      and mist
  echoing
      from mountaintops
       from fields of winter
       and the river.

I Write

I write to understand,

my pen is my teacher.

It is through the wisdom of my pen

another voice speaks

the voice is clear and knowing.

I write to understand

    I write to honor

        to forgive

            to remember.

My Teachers

Thank you to my husband, Jim Donaldson

Thank you to our Family

Thank you to my Mother and my Father

Thank you to my Brother and my Sisters

Thank you to my Teachers

Clara Haaheim

Wanda Orton

Pesha Gertler

Ron Allen

Doris Toppen Northstrom